DEPROGRAMMIN

A Companion Volume to *QUICKSAND*

CONTENTS

INTRODUCTION

In my 371-page paperback, I described the nightmare of 12-Step programs. It included many of my own experiences, experiences related by others, and references to material by experts and professionals in the fields of addiction, recovery, and cults. What many of us learned, though, was leaving the programs was not the end of it. While there can be much "wreckage," one category is described as the need to "deprogram." Although I made a half-hearted, on-my-own attempt quite a few years ago, it accomplished nothing. More recently, I began to find back-up from others who had left the programs-- not only the need to address common problems, but the need to find useful solutions. That is the reason I decided to write this "companion volume" to *Quicksand.*

We can start with this particular terminology.

First, a dictionary defines *deprogramming* as "to release someone from apparent brainwashing, typically that of a religious cult, by the systematic reindoctrination of conventional values." If you have not yet read *Quicksand,* you may be surprised to see words such as 'brainwashing,' 'indoctrinating,' and 'cults' when describing 12-Step programs. If you doubt that these terms are related to 12-Step programs, read *Quicksand*-- including, but not limited to, material from a wide range of experts and professionals.

Second, a dictionary defines *indoctrinate* as "to teach someone to fully accept the ideas, opinions, and beliefs of a particular group, and to not consider other ideas, opinions, and beliefs."

Furthering this, synonyms for *indoctrinate* are listed as including: *brainwash, propagandize, reeducate, convince, persuade, mold, program, condition.*

I'd venture to say anyone who has 'escaped' 12-Step programs-- and 12-Step program influences-- would consider all of those terms to be completely accurate, and completely in tune with their experiences. The problem: as with all other wreckage, it does not disappear on its own. Even if you never return to a 12-Step meeting, and cut off contact with all 12-Step program members, it will remain until you take action to do something about it.

I recall the first time I heard the word 'indoctrinate.' It had nothing to do with 12-Step programs. One day, many years ago, I was participating in a fund-raising event with one of my kids, aged eleven. A college student who was studying to be a minister was in charge of the event, and appeared surprised when the youngster stepped backward quietly and politely as he prepared to lead a prayer before lunch. "You don't believe in indoctrinating children?" he asked. I replied I did not-- and didn't elaborate on my viewpoint that even children have their own minds.

However, a 12-Step program is not a casual prayer in someone's back yard. *Indoctrinating* does indeed include all of those synonyms-- and more.

There are a variety of approaches used within the programs, and by individual members. I will address some of the most common in this book, along with some solutions you can think about.

In this introduction, though, there are a couple of approaches that should leave no doubt in your mind that *deprogramming* is essential if you want a quality life-- free from 12-Step influences *and* their effects on you.

The first approach may actually be the first you heard when you attended your initial meeting or spoke with a 12-Step program member for the first time. One common saying is *act as if;* a similar common saying is *fake it 'til you make it.*

There are two parts to this approach. One is you are expected to say things about yourself that you do not believe, or know to not be true. The next part is the reactions of program members, depending on whether or not you 'cooperate.' If you say what they want you to say, you are likely to receive a variety of positive reinforcements. In contrast, if you do not cooperate, you will receive a variety of negative reactions. The purpose: if you say something untrue often enough, it is possible you will begin to believe it yourself.

Although I never fell into the trap of believing untrue things myself, I certainly experienced this form of indoctrination. As they were 12-Step programs, there was extreme pressure for individuals to describe themselves as 'alcoholics' or 'addicts,' even when they were not. And this form of indoctrination covers much more than alcoholism and drug addiction. They expect-- no, *insist*-- that people lie about themselves, and everything about their lives.

A second approach involves individuals with no knowledge or authority claiming they know more about you and every aspect of your life than you yourself, your family members, and even professionals such as health care providers. It includes everything from 'diagnosing' health conditions to attempting to cause you to 'remember' incidents in your past that never happened. The most unscrupulous NRA's attempt to weaken people by getting people to doubt everything about themselves and others in their lives.

When NRA's are through with you-- if they ever are-- you may have reached the point of not even knowing who you are anymore. Equally destructive-- if not more so-- they can take the same approaches to your family members or other loved ones.

Similar to any other *cult,* the effects and after-effects vary from person to person. This should not be surprising, as every person is a unique individual. Similar to any other cult, a person can be a fully participating member while functioning normally in his everyday life, or not being able to function at all. And similar to any other cult, separating oneself from these so-called 'fellowships' can be a process that ranges from difficult to extremely complicated.

If you are attempting to free yourself from the influences of 12-Step programs, this little book can help. However, you should not try to do it all alone. Find people in your everyday life who understand and support what you are going through, network with others who have had the same experiences, and do not hesitate to seek professional help if you are experiencing serious problems with resolving issues connected to your involvement with 12-Step programs.

As for those who have applied the strongest, most negative influence and pressure, I will use the same term I used throughout *Quicksand-- NRA's--* to describe this segment of the 12-Step program population. *Non-recovered alcoholics/addicts* is my term for the many individuals who care nothing about 'recovery,' but are involved in these programs for the purpose of harming and exploiting other people. And while there are many individuals in the programs who are not in this category, the countless numbers who do exist in the programs make these books necessary.

FREE WILL: A GIFT FROM GOD

Sometimes, reading about something does not have the degree of impact as encountering it in person. This was the case when I first encountered an odd, and potentially dangerous, approach to human will.

As you may know, the terms "God" and "Higher Power" occur frequently throughout 12-Step program literature. At first glance, an individual is advised to apply these terms to 'the God of his understanding.' However, as with any other aspect of the 12-Step programs, one's first glance is often not what one finds afterward.

This particular encounter involved an individual in a sponsor/sponsee relationship. Although the programs acknowledge many people do not have a specific 'higher power,' that was not even the case in this instance. While the sponsee belonged to a mainstream religion, he was still advised to take a different approach. Rather than using the terms 'God' and 'Higher Power' to reflect the God he claimed to believe in, his sponsor told him to replace those terms with the sponsor's name.

Examples were given: *"Joe,* grant me the serenity....," "Praying for the knowledge of *Joe's* will," etc.

My first and immediate reaction was *"Where have I heard this before-- why does it sound familiar?"* What came to mind was Charles Manson and his followers. Specifically, there had been an interview where one of his followers commented on how Manson had changed his middle name to 'Willis,' and repeated this new name for emphasis: *"Charles' Will.. is... man's son."* In other words, he was presenting himself-- and his 'will'-- to be one and the same as God. And that's precisely what came to mind when the young sponsee related his sponsor's approach.

Equally important, other meeting-goers did not object. In fact, they agreed wholeheartedly with this approach. In one meeting, for example, when the sponsee began reciting The Serenity Prayer with the sponsor's name in place of the name 'God,' individuals in the meeting cheered and applauded.

Naturally, this approach can be damaging and destructive under any circumstances. In this particular instance, though, it was made worse by the low-class beliefs about status and authority. Worse yet, the sponsor could accurately be described as a "bug-eyed, ranting madman," who, like all who have "Jekyll-and-Hyde" abilities, could appear "smooth and polished" *when it benefited him to do so.* In other words, the sponsor was perfectly in control of his approaches and behaviors, using whatever would benefit him the most in any given situation.

A second approach involved a sponsor who claimed to not have any 'Higher Power.' Stating she had not yet decided whether she believed in God or not, she expressed her opinion that the Steps and Stepwork were not only unnecessary, but foolish. Instead, her approach to her sponsees and general members was as if they were all her personal psychology project. As only one example: *"You're in the crisis/awakening stage."*

Look at it this way-- and this should make your blood curl: your sponsor is no more and no less than an alcoholic and/or drug addict in a 12-Step program- do you really want to consider the individual to be '*a power greater than yourself'?*

While these two examples show the degree of power, and how power can be misused, a third approach is equally mindboggling: individuals are told they can use *inanimate objects* as their 'higher powers.' If you are like most people, you probably have lightbulbs and chairs in your home. Would you believe a "chair" can 'grant you serenity,' or 'pray for the knowledge of a "lightbulb's" will'?

What is the purpose of this outrageous approach? When an individual is presented this as an option, he may initially have a false sense of security-- making the mistake of believing he is actually in charge of his own choices. However, if he continues participating in the program, he will see how quickly NRA's attempt to sway his beliefs so his beliefs are in-tune with theirs.

These approaches may seem completely out-of-line, but if you read through some of the program literature you will see parts of it is addressed. An individual is told if he does not have a 'higher power,' he can consider his sponsor, his 12-Step group, or the program itself *to be* his higher power. As the way it is presented appears to be nothing more than a method for newcomers to get through confusion and uncertainty in their earliest days in the program, a closer look shows it is not nearly so useful or harmless.

You can begin by applying this suggestion to the Steps, stepwork, and The Serenity Prayer. One example that should make everything perfectly clear: "turn my will and my life over to the care of *my sponsor*" (or *the group* or *The Program*). Although this can result in limitless damage and destruction if 'sponsor' is power-crazed, has personal motives, etc., it is not even appropriate when one is fortunate enough to have a sponsor who does not have those characteristics.

There are many components that make up a human being. The *will* is one of those components. The *will* is considered to be the component that accounts for personal choice and self-determination. It involves such attributes as the ability to consent, refuse, decide, desire; and, in its proper state, is accompanied by one's conscience.

The pressure to turn your will and your life over to someone else can have a number of repercussions. You are becoming *dependent* on someone else-- not for help or guidance, but to take over that which you have surrendered. Paraphrasing a quote by Dr. Martin Luther King, Jr., you can no longer assume responsibility for yourself as a human being. Surrendering your will means you lack one of the most basic components that make you a human being.

The catch: you do not need to buy into this nonsense in order to be affected by it. Even if you do not verbally or consciously 'surrender your will,' participating in the 12-Step programs means consistent, ongoing pressure to leave your 'will' further and further behind. From the most minute aspects of your life to the most important, you will find less and less of it is in your own hands. You will find personal choice and self-determination begin to disappear-- and may eventually be obliterated entirely.

Each person has his or her own beliefs that pertain to this subject. As the term 'God' often appears in these discussions of human will, we can begin there. When you look at the human will as a gift from God, what you are pressured to do is to throw this gift back, figuratively saying *"I do not want it."* Obviously, that is not the right approach. God does not want you to be less than a human being-- which is why you were born with a will in the first place. And if your beliefs-system involves a higher power that is not God, or no higher power at all, it is still not in your best interest to throw away your own will.

You cannot adequately function as a human being without your own will. While this is a logical point, consider the topic even further: who, exactly, are you surrendering your will *to?* Do you really believe he, she, or they should take over your ability to consent, refuse, decide, desire, choose? Do you really believe individuals whose main difference from yourself is they have spent years or decades sitting in 12-Step meetings are in any way qualified to assume these abilities for you-- rather than you having and doing it yourself? And, equally important, who will you *be* when you no longer have one of the most essential components of a human being?

Think about it: depending on your age and location, you may or may not remember the large flock of misguided young people who gave up their free wills and their consciences in favor of "Charles' Will." It is no less destructive for *your* free will and conscience to be 'surrendered' to a sponsor, a 12-Step group, or The Program-- or to watch it slip away, slowly but surely, from Program influences.

Think about it very carefully: if you would not 'surrender your will' to Charles Manson or a stranger you see walking down the street, it is no more in your best interests to take that approach to a sponsor, a 12-Step group, or a program.

In fact, if you are a reasonable, rational person, you would not even 'surrender' your will and your life-- your self-determination, your ability to consent, refuse, decide, desire, choose-- to people in your life whom you love and know are trustworthy, such as a parent, spouse, or child. The reason:

because you are a human being, and one's *will* is an essential part of a human being.

Do not give it away, nor allow it to be taken away from you. And if you already have-- *reclaim what is rightfully yours.*

"SPECIAL KNOWLEDGE"

As you may already know, there is much about 12-Step programs that is harmful and potentially dangerous. An additional point to consider is it pales in comparison to much that finds its way into the programs while having nothing to do with the 12-Step programs. It includes topics and approaches that are not condoned by the programs, and the only references you will find in the program literature are warnings *against* these topics and approaches. One that bears special noting is the subject of "special knowledge;" the term "inside information" can also apply.

Despite the programs' admonishment that it is something no one in a 12-Step program can do, the programs are filled with NRA's who do it anyway. Although I had countless experiences with the topic throughout the years, there was one in particular that did not occur to me until quite recently. Specifically, what did not occur to me was the logical question: when NRA's claim to have 'special knowledge' or 'inside information,' *how do they claim to have come by* such knowledge or information? And whether individuals on the receiving end of an NRA's lies believe they are telling the truth or know they are lying, that is the question that should be asked.

Looking back at my experiences, there is an answer: NRA's who claim to have special knowledge or inside information *misrepresent themselves,* and *misrepresent situations.* And it is with these misrepresentations NRA's attempt to lead others to believe the lies they tell.

The incident that led me to wonder how NRA's can consistently present false information: one NRA concocted a sh*tload of lies to damage my reputation; amongst her lies was the tale that my youngster was living on nothing but "Vienna Sausages and Cheez-Whiz," because I was not providing decent food for my family.

To clarify with the facts: I was spending more than $400. per month on groceries for my family; I, or a combination of us, shopped regularly; the little cottage we lived in was stocked with a full refrigerator and food closets; and good meals were on the table at mealtimes. In addition, I didn't purchase non-kosher food-- and "Vienna Sausages" are pork products.

The catch about these facts: the NRA had no way of knowing any of this. Obviously, as she and her boyfriend had never been in our home, and I never ran into them in a grocery store, they had no way of knowing our shopping or eating habits. The catch that is even more relevant, though: when they were concocting this lie, how did they claim they *did?* Although this logical question didn't occur to me at the time, it seems it should have occurred to *somebody.*

Common to all the NRA's who told lies for their own personal gain, they misrepresented themselves, and they misrepresented situations. While I do not know what they said to a wide range of other people, one individual made the comment *"I thought they were your friends!"* In other words, individuals were led to believe the NRA's had been longtime, good friends of mine, and, thus, *'knew all about'* me; while the fact was I had never met either of them before we arrived in their city.

This deceptive approach of leading others to believe NRA's 'know all about you' is common. In this situation, as well as others, NRA's lied about how they came to be in my life-- how long they had known me, how well they had known me, and the relationships they had with me. While in each and every instance in which this type of deception occurred the NRA's in question were strangers who had never even met me before, others were led to believe they had 'inside information' or 'special knowledge' about me.

However, special knowledge and inside information is not limited to information NRA's do not have, but claim to have, about specific individuals. It covers other topics as well. Not only do NRA's claim to have knowledge and information about *people,* but on a wide variety of other subjects, too.

One common example involves NRA's who attempt to replace professionals. Although 12-Step program literature warns about this, there are many who do it anyway. Not only did I have numerous experiences with this issue myself, I have known a considerable number of other people who had similar experiences. At the top of the list are NRA's who apply undue influence and pressure to stop others from seeking and following health care advice and/or treatment from legitimate health care providers.

Regardless of one's opinion on 12-Step programs in general, this topic is only one example of NRA's who *do not care what their own programs say.* And whether it is for the purpose of feeding their egos, gaining power over other people, or any other reason, the reason is not nearly as important as the consequences. NRA's who practice medicine without a license, and violate other people's rights, can destroy people's health and lives.

On one side of the issue are NRA's who come between individuals and the individuals' health care providers. An example I have heard time and time again: NRA's who pressure individuals to not take medications prescribed by, or recommended by, their own doctors. Examples I have heard included pain medication for a person who had cancer, cold medication for someone with the flu, psychiatric medications for individuals with clinical depression, and antibiotics prescribed for a person who had a strep infection. These individuals were all told they must ignore their doctors' advice, and do what 'sponsor' says instead. In the latter instance, the person was told he must 'treat' the strep infection by eating licorice. I have known numerous instances of medical problems and mental health problems worsening because individuals must ignore their doctors and do what the sponsor says instead.

On the other side of the issue are NRA's who, instead of telling individuals to ignore legitimate health care advice, claim they know 'more and better' than qualified health care providers.

From medical conditions to mental health issues, NRA's claim they, rather than health care providers, can make 'diagnoses.' Similar to NRA's who claim they 'know all about' individual people by misrepresenting themselves and misrepresenting situations, NRA's who portray themselves as suitable substitutes for health care providers also misrepresent themselves and misrepresent situations. While NRA's who attempt to come between individuals and their health care providers often resort to bullying, others misrepresent themselves and misrepresent situations by nothing more than reading a book, seeing something on the internet, or taking a class-- using a few words they learned here or there to convince others that they are an authority on the subject. While they have no real knowledge, education, or credentials, they attempt to cause people to believe they are more knowledgeable than legitimate health care providers who went through many years of education and earned degrees in their particular field.

One of the most outrageous examples involved an NRA who claimed he 'knew at least eight people' in his small city who had 'multiple-personality disorders.' Not only dismissing what modern science says on the topic, and dismissing what his own 'program' says about the scope of a 12-Step program, the individual who did not even make it into high school claimed he could 'diagnose' such conditions. When asked if mental health professionals had stated the people had such issues, he replied that he and only he could make diagnoses.

Program literature itself warns against these behaviors, and informs the reader of the literature that no one in a program is an 'expert' on anything. In the rare instances in which one may meet an actual professional in a program, there is the caution that professional advice is not within the scope of a 12-Step program-- that the entire scope of a program is assisting people in their attempts to recover from alcohol or drug addiction. Personally, I encountered a couple of physicians and attorneys in 12-Step programs, and these individuals did not try to circumvent what was taught by their programs. The majority, though, do not have such credentials-- from my experiences, they ranged from students to drop-outs.

Ego-trips, power-trips, or manipulation just because they can-- the reasons are not nearly as relevant as the consequences. NRA's who claim they have special knowledge or inside information that you do not have about yourself, or that they know 'more and better' than health care providers, or that you cannot use a medication given to you by your own physician, are ignoring what is taught by their own 12-Step programs. They are 'playing games' with your health, your mind, your life.

Such individuals can sarcastically be referred to as 'armchair experts'-- with no legitimate knowledge, they claim to be experts on every topic that exists. As one ridiculous example, an NRA insisted it takes exactly 'fifty minutes' for roadways to be safe after a rainstorm. Allegedly, road surfaces, temperatures, and other relevant factors did not figure into it. I knew better than this in my high school driver's education class.

When it comes to the most serious and controversial topic, though, 'armchair experts' endanger people's health and lives. And most important, it shows the clear difference between NRA's and individuals who are truly interested in recovery and better lives. One NRA, for example, said no one who is given anything by their doctors should ever take it-- because it 'blocks their recovery.'

They dismiss what their own programs say in order to feed their own egos. You may even have heard NRA's tell you *the program says* this is the correct approach. The catch: not only do the program *not* say this, they say the exact opposite. In fact, the two most well-known 12-Step programs for individuals with substance abuse problems actually have special pamphlets addressing this issue because it is so serious and widespread. It is one issue on which both programs take a sensible approach.

In their pamphlets devoted to health issues, AA and NA both state while individuals with substance abuse problems may be prone to misusing medications, correct use of medications for legitimate conditions does not constitute 'relapsing,' 'blowing one's sobriety,' or 'not working the program.' And even more to the point, both AA and NA caution alcoholics and addicts to discuss their health issues frankly and honestly *with their own physicians--* and that sponsors, oldtimers, and other members should never "play doctor."

In contrast, NRA's with no authority and no credentials do exactly that. On health care and virtually every other topic in existence, it's all a matter of *"Look at how important I am... Look at how much power I have! I have other people's lives in my hands!"*

"HOSTAGE SITUATIONS"

When it came to 12-Step programs and individuals in the programs, the main reason for my confusion was nothing I encountered was like anything I had ever encountered before. An additional, connected subject, though, was the vocabulary. Although the odd and unfamiliar vocabulary I began encountering was on a wide range of topics, one topic was what an NRA referred to as *'hostage situations.'*

During those years, I experienced it in a number of different ways, from a number of different NRA's. One approach came to my attention as being quite common in the programs-- not only for me, but others as well. Whether the term is used or implied, NRA's who create 'hostage situations' often do so by approaching a person they wish to influence or dominate, and attempt to cause that person to *distrust* others.

If you fall into the trap that the only individual you can 'trust' is the NRA-- that he or she is honest, trustworthy, and looking out for your best interests, while 'others' are not-- you may fall further into the trap by distrusting other people, not listening to other people when they present opposing information, or avoiding other people entirely. While I, personally, never bought into this nonsense, numerous NRA's did their damned best to try to create hostage situations-- isolation, where I'd have no frame-of-reference but *theirs.*

One NRA comes to mind. I was new in the city, and did not know anyone. Because of this, the NRA pestered and pestered me to accompany her to a 12-Step meeting. In addition, while I did not understand her reasons at the time, she began insisting I must attend meetings regularly-- that there was no such thing as attending too many meetings, and that it must be my number-one priority. (Included in this was her insistence that I should not look for a job, should not stop smoking cigarettes, and should place my entire focus on attending meetings. I later learned all of this was due to the NRA portraying me to the locals as a 'low, desperate Addict who could not get clean'-- while I was not even a drug user at all).

The catch: while the NRA was insisting my entire focus must be on attending 12-Step meetings, they had to be meetings *where she was present.* I was told to not go to meetings unless she was the leader, or at least was attending. To this end, she began with a tale about one of the regulars at a local meeting. She said I shouldn't go to the meeting unless she was present, because this man would *'molest'* me; she added he had *'molested all the women'* who went to that meeting. Unfamiliar with this approach, I envisioned some kind of wild-eyed pervert. That was not what I found when I entered the meeting. Instead, I found a frail, elderly man who threw friendly bear-hugs around the women who approached him. Equally important, the women I witnessed did not object to this behavior. Yet, to the NRA, it was perfectly acceptable to claim a terminally-ill man 'molested' women-- believing this would scare me away from attending any meetings without her.

She then proceeded to tell me everything that was 'wrong' with the other meetings in the area, assuming it would stop me from going to meetings she did not attend. As one example, she claimed the group leader's small child wrecked the meetings by running around the room loudly, and bothering people. She said I should not want to waste my time at those meetings. As another example, she described one meetingplace as 'a lesbian meeting,' telling me I should not want to be in a roomful of lesbians. On and on this went-- there was something 'wrong' with every meeting except hers, and something 'wrong' with virtually everyone who attended the meetings.

As is the case with NRA's, she had a reason for wanting a hostage situation. If I followed her demands, anything I ever said in a meeting would be said in her presence. If I followed her demands, nothing I did or said would be without her knowledge. And, equally destructive in this particular situation, she and the NRA she was living with could count on many opportunities to lie about and discredit me behind my back-- long before they began doing it to my face. When my work hours expanded so I rarely had time for any meetings, these NRA's took full advantage of my absence.

Over the years, there were a number of experiences with hostage situations. I experienced situations where I was trapped by threats, and by force. However, not only was that particular NRA's method very common, it shows the extremes individuals with wrongful motives will go to to get what they want, and to come out on top.

Years later, her method reappeared in a different city. Again I was new to an area, and a 12-Step meeting is one place I should not have been. Again I was approached with tales about why I should go out of my way to avoid "others." I was told 'most of the guys are predators and perpetrators and rapists; and most of the women are criminals, lesbians, bisexuals, and prostitutes.' Later I was told individuals I'd met were 'serial killers' and 'in the business of murder.'

Although there were other aspects to the hostage situation, when I did not buy into this nonsense I found the NRA was taking my absence to employ the same tactics as the previously-mentioned NRA: attempting to convince people I did not know well or did not know at all that I was a horrible, messed-up person.

Nor was that the extent of it. First, I was told there were numerous individuals in the meetings monitoring me on his behalf-- assisting the NRA in stalking and harassment when he was not present to do it himself. Next, I was told all the people at the meetings had so much misinformation about me and disliked me so intensely that I should never go back to the meetings at all. (On a side note: while the NRA acknowledged to me that he knew I wasn't an alcoholic, at the same time he was telling others that I was a 'dry-drunk alcoholic in denial,' and 'so messed-up that I'd flip my wig permanently'- *yet* going to every extreme possible to keep me away from other people and the meetings. "You don't need any of those people- all you need is *me!*" he said.

The purpose: so I could not approach anyone for help, and so he could continue to lie behind my back.

Not only did I have plenty of experiences with hostage situations myself, and various other people who managed to 'escape' the 12-Step programs related similar experiences, I also witnessed it on a number of occasions. In one instance, for example, I overheard a conversation where a much-older NRA was attempting to create distrust in a much-younger newcomer. *"Don't trust any of those people- you can't trust any of them!"*

In some cases, it is a warped desire for power; in others, there is something much more serious and important they wish to accomplish or gain at someone else's expense.

However, there are many negative points you may find in 12-Step programs that are very similar to Domestic Violence situations-- and "hostage situations" are one similarity. From my own experiences, as well as those I was told and witnessed, the specifics are not relevant. An NRA can be older or younger than yourself, male or female, and you do not need to have any kind of personal relationship with them. Speaking from my own experiences, the NRA's who took this approach were all strangers-- individuals whom I had just met and did not know. Yet they attempted to create distrust, and claim 'power in my life.'

Similar to domestic violence, such situations are about *power,* they are about *dominating and control,* and whether it involves physical attacks or verbal threats, it is *abuse.* And whether NRA's who practice these kinds of power-ploys are seeking to gain something by isolating and weakening you-- as the NRA's I encountered in three different locations-- or are simply employing these tactics because they *can,* it is just as vile and disgusting as the kinds of trash who commit acts of violence against women and/or children.

From my experiences, though, there is a difference: NRA's in 12-Step programs *are nothing to you.* If they commit these types of acts against you, they are nothing more nor less than criminals. And while individuals who commit acts of domestic violence are criminals, too, you should have an even stronger standing against NRA's because NRA's have no place in your life.

If you are like me, you have "gut instincts" that work and are accurate. If someone has tried to manipulate you into believing he/she is the only person you can trust, wants to monopolize your time, and/or tries to isolate you from other people, your gut instincts should tell you there is something very, very wrong. Not only are hostage situations a matter of power, but it is an especially insidious form of power that no one should have over another person. And these behaviors are proof that such individuals have no interest in 'recovery' or 'change.'

The point: if you are an adult, lawful liberty, freedom, and independence are your rights. In fact, to some degree, these rights even extend to children. Do not allow power-seeking NRA's in 12-Step programs to infringe upon your rights or take them away.

PROOFTEXTING AND OTHER NO-NO'S

One practice common amongst the fringe-element known as 'fundamentalists' is a practice known as *"prooftexting."* This topic must be addressed, as it is also common in 12-Step programs. Prooftexting involves a) taking a statement, passage, or quotation out of context, and b) proceeding to tell others what the statement, passage, or quotation *"really* means." It is, without a doubt, the height of arrogance.

An additional problem with this practice is individuals are often led to believe the statements, passages, or quotations are actually part of the 12-Step programs. Not only are the original sources and contexts dismissed entirely, NRA's in the programs attempt to convince others that *they know* the true meanings. If you have been in or around the programs, you have probably heard sources as diverse as Joan Baez and Albert Einstein quoted out of context, with what they actually said "tailored" for the sake of the program or individuals in the program.

One in particular bears noting, as you have surely heard, seen, or read it at some point in time. It is known as "The Serenity Prayer." However, you are less likely to have heard the original version, or been informed of the source. First, the individual who was credited for writing the original 12-Step book "modified it." And second, true to fundamentalist form, you may have heard 12-Step program members "explain its *true* meaning."

A theologian named Reinhold Niebuhr produced this to include in one of his sermons:

> God, give me grace to accept with serenity
> the things that cannot be changed,
> Courage to change the things
> which should be changed,
> and the Wisdom to distinguish
> the one from the other.
>
> Living one day at a time,
> Enjoying one moment at a time,
> Accepting hardship as a pathway to peace,
> Taking, as Jesus did,
> This sinful world as it is,
> Not as I would have it,
> Trusting that You will make all things right,
> If I surrender to Your will,
> So that I may be reasonably happy in this life,
> And supremely happy with You forever in the next.
>
> Amen.

There may be a number of reasons you object to this little poem. As you can see, it does not uphold the claim that everyone in 12-Step programs are free to have 'the God of his understanding.' It does not uphold the claim that 12-Step programs 'are spiritual, not religious.' However, it is the prooftexting that should be considered especially objectionable. NRA's do not take it as Niebuhr wrote and meant it, but as *they* mean it.

One example came in a 12-Step meeting I attended. When it was one individual's turn to "share," he decided to use the time to "explain what it *really* means." Using the modified form common within the program, he proceeded to state: "the things we cannot change: *Other People.* The things we can change: *Ourselves.* " And whether you agree with this approach or not, consider the way it fits into 12-Step programs: their ongoing message of *Powerlessness,* and, equally destructive, *Acceptance.*

Considering the ongoing pressure NRA's apply to others in attempts to *change* everything about others, it is almost humorous. The way it promotes these destructive messages, though, does nothing but weaken people even further. There is certainly much about "other people" that we cannot and should not attempt to change, but there is also much we should not simply 'accept.'

A second part of the sermon should also be of interest to former program members. If you read what Niebuhr said about surrendering to God's will, it is much different from what you find in the programs-- including the Steps. Depending on your religion or beliefs, surrendering to God's will may be a good thing-- *but Niebuhr does not say* you should surrender *your* will to God. And it certainly does not say you should surrender your will to a 12-Step program or individuals therein.

So whether you are talking about a 12-Step program or individuals in the program, this prooftexting is yet another way they twist everything apart for their own purposes. Whether they are quoting or misquoting from the Bible, historical figures, pop music, or anywhere else, NRA's assert they know "more, better, and different" than the individuals who actually wrote it.

"THEY DON'T PAY MUCH ATTENTION TO 'BILL,' DO THEY?"

If you read 12-Step literature, one topic you will find addressed throughout some of the books covers individuals who use what they learn in the programs to harm and exploit others. It is said that while many individuals use 'every trick available' when they are coping with active addiction, there are also many who continue the same approach within the 12-Step programs. In other words, unlike people who proceed to true recovery, these types of individuals-- NRA's-- continue seeking ways to have 'an edge' over others.

While the topic can cover virtually every subject in existence, one in particular did not occur to me until quite recently. Specifically, it is an approach NRA's often use to *twist* approaches found in their own 12-Step literature. And the subject goes all the way back to the original 12-Step book.

Whether we agree or disagree with the 12-Step book, its purported author presents his view on two related issues. First, his belief that alcoholics who have 'found the path to recovery' should put no stops in trying to reach out to help those who have not found it. Second, he described the situations in which a person was likely to find such 'candidates': there were individuals whose alcoholism was extreme enough to have landed them in the hospital, either as the result of drinking binges or what is commonly known as "the DT's."

The purported author of the book referred to such individuals as *"sick."* In fact, individuals who were hospitalized with delirium tremens, or as the result of drinking binges, were not only physically and mentally in poor condition, but could even have been ill enough that it threatened their lives.

As such, he recommended an approach: if the individual the reader wished to help was uncooperative, the reader should solicit assistance from the individual's family. On a side note: as the alcoholics in question were male, he advised his readers to approach their wives, inform the wives how ill their husbands were, and inform them the best course of action would be to get those men into the 12-Step program.

I, and many others who related their own experiences, found something entirely different-- and the differences occurred with *both* issues.

Speaking from my own experiences, the numerous examples in which I heard the term 'sick' had nothing to do with alcoholism (or drug addiction). Instead, they were nothing more than responses to NRA's not getting their own way. The first example was a clear illustration of how NRA's intentionally misuse the term for their own purposes. The situation: I expressed reservations about making a radical move that was not in my best interests-- not only leaving nearly everything and everyone behind, moving to a new location where I did not know anyone, and having not a cent to my name in doing so, but being pressured to do this. I am sure most sensible people would have had the same reservations-- even moving to a new location under the best circumstances requires careful planning, knowing what one can reasonably expect in the new environment, etc. However, I was told that not simply cooperating with what I was asked to do meant I was 'sick.' And I have experienced the same manipulation with a variety of NRA's over the years.

The second part of the approach can be more dangerous. Unlike what the 12-Step book says about soliciting assistance from wives to get seriously ill men into the programs, there are NRA's who go after families for other reasons-- *their own* reasons. Instead of 'your husband who is in the hospital due to alcohol abuse needs help from a 12-Step program,' you may find NRA's who go after spouses, children, siblings, etc., with entirely different motives.

And the most important point to keep in mind is if you yourself cannot grasp the underhandedness of NRA's, your family members certainly cannot. What I mean by that is even if you have some degree of experience with NRA's in 12-Step programs, it is not likely your family members have had such experience. And while this leads your family members to be defenseless against the tactics of NRA's, you are even more defenseless when your family members are pulled into it. Even the most intelligent people cannot recognize what is often referred to as "stranger danger" when the 'strangers' appear to be in your life or you are in theirs.

If you have become a target of this type of NRA, it is nothing like the situations presented in the 12-Step book. You are not likely to be hospitalized due to alcohol or drug abuse; you do not even need to be an alcoholic or an addict at all. Whether you do not have any substance abuse problems, or are making progress with your own recovery, NRA's not only misrepresent themselves but misrepresent *you*. Depending on your particular situation, you may find NRA's who approach your spouse or significant other, child, parent, sibling, or other family member, falsely presenting themselves as kind, caring individuals who only want to 'help' you-- while presenting *you* as someone who is hopelessly and helplessly 'sick.'

There are a variety of ways this can occur. You can look at it as NRA's use any and every opportunity they find, and if there is no opportunity they can create one. One example of the former involves 12-Step groups that encourage people to bring their families to meetings, activities, and other events. In addition to regular meetings and celebrations for 'clean and/or sober' anniversaries, there are holiday parties, picnics, dances, sports teams, and so forth. While it may be presented as expecting your family members to 'be supportive of your recovery,' that is not the issue at all. Instead, it gives them the message that the individuals they meet have a legitimate place in your life, that they are all trustworthy, that they are all your friends. And it gives NRA's who do not meet those descriptions the opportunity to meet and take advantage of them.

A second example involves the approach of taking on 12-Step members as everything from your 'social network' to your 'support system.' In fact, if you ask 12-Step program members, you are likely to find the people they associate with outside 12-Step meetings are almost exclusively other program members. While this is an unfair burden to family members and true friends, it has the potential to be even more destructive. Simply

27

because you have met someone at a 12-Step meeting, it does not mean the individual should be in your personal life, your home, or around your family. Yet NRA's can use every tactic available to them to access your personal life, your home, and your family anyway.

However, a third example is even more extreme. Using the twist on the 12-Step book, you may find NRA's go after your family without your knowledge. And, as I stated earlier, it is not about trying to get families to see a 'person hospitalized with the DT's' needs assistance.' As you may have read in the References section of *Quicksand,* it is a tactic abusers often use: using one's family members as leverage to get what they want.

When I was doing research for *Quicksand,* many individuals told their heartbreaking stories of how their families were put under undue strain, and some even permanently torn apart, because of NRA's. Pitting family members against each other, urging people to cut their family members out of their lives, and attempting to claim knowledge and authority that they did not have, were some of the most common examples. When they belonged to the programs, they were urged to 'trust' other program members instead of their own families, and their families were urged to 'trust' NRA's instead of *them.*

Using 'pop-psych' terminology, NRA's who take these approaches have an *"agenda."* They are never acting in the best interest of anyone they involve in their scams. Not only are they using human beings for whatever goal they have of their own, they are using what they learned in their own programs to do it. And this is one of the main differences between individuals who are interested in recovery, and NRA's who have no such interest.

While individuals-- in and out of 12-Step programs-- may offer genuine assistance to people who are struggling with substance-abuse problems, this is no concern to NRA's. The way they attempt to tear apart other people's families shows they have no interest in 'recovery.'

"I HATE SPINACH- DO YOU?"

Whatever your opinion may be of the 12-Step programs, there is one point that should be perfectly clear: there is much that occurs within the programs that is by no means condoned by the programs themselves. One of the most common examples is the emphasis NRA's place on *"the past"*-- not in the context of 'recovery,' but as a means to manipulate and exploit others.

If you read the 12-Step program books thoroughly, you will find 'the past' addressed in a much different context. The general viewpoint is one's past is something one must look at, see for what it was, and move on. This viewpoint is even addressed in a number of the "steps."

In contrast, you may find the subject is used by NRA's to weaken individuals. Rather than mistakes one must make up for, and difficult experiences one must heal from, one of the most insidious approaches used by NRA's is the approach that *you do not even know what happened in your own life.*

A human being has personal preferences, likes and dislikes, and free will. To an NRA, you are not a human being-- because you lack these characteristics. Dismissing the fact that even small children have these characteristics, NRA's take the approach to adults of all ages that these characteristics do not exist. Instead, they will claim 'it is all about *the past.'*

We can look at a comparison that can have basis in fact. If, for example, a person is bitten by a dog when he is a youngster, he may grow up to dislike or fear dogs. However, amongst NRA's who wish to manipulate others, it is not about this logical conclusion. Instead, you will find NRA's asserting that you would never dislike or object to anything unless 'something in your past' led you to dislike or object to it.

A common theme amongst manipulative NRA's is that if there is no logical conclusion to be drawn, there must be something that happened that you simply do not remember. Taking a cue from decades ago, before scientific research proved "repressed memories" rarely occur, you may hear that all sorts of 'traumas' occurred in your past that never actually occurred at all.

What exactly is the purpose of this type of manipulation? From my experiences, there can be a number of purposes, and they can affect both the individual himself and other people who are in or around his life. If an individual falls into this trap, he may begin doubting everything about himself-- after all, you must be a very weak and sick person if you do not even remember your own life history. Now, if you can even imagine the consequences of something like this: an NRA who can manipulate a person into believing he does not even have the facts about his own life history *has that person exactly where he wants him.*

On the other side of the issue: such an individual is portrayed to others as weak, sick, and unstable-- after all, an individual who does not even know the facts about his own life history must be a very messed-up person indeed. At its most extreme, other people will stop believing in you, and stop trusting you. After all, if you can have years or decades worth of 'repressed memories,' nothing you do or say should be considered truthful or accurate.

The catch: not only is this 'it's all about the past' approach not a part of the 12-Step programs, it has no factual basis at all. As most people who were adults at the time may remember, this so-called mass hysteria began with a legal case that occurred in California in the mid-1980's. Suddenly, healthy stable adults across America began to claim 'recovered memories.' And while extensive research concluded 'repressed memories' rarely occur, NRA's continue to take great liberties in exploiting people who are not aware of the facts.

Many individuals who managed to 'escape' the programs went on to describe this tactic as "They rewrite your life history." You can check references in *Quicksand* and find various experts who spent many years researching cults describing it as a common occurrence in cults.

From my experiences, there is an additional factor that must be addressed. Of all the NRA's who attempted to 'rewrite my life history,' there was one very important factor they had in common: all of these NRA's were individuals whom I had just met; they were total strangers who knew nothing about my actual 'life history.' Yet, similar to the topics and approaches addressed in the 'Special Knowledge' section, they claimed they had knowledge and information about people that the people did not have about themselves.

However, while that may be the most important factor, there is another to consider: of all the former program members who have 'shared' in ongoing detail about their experiences in the 12-Step programs, there was not a one who did not have this experience. In other words, NRA's everywhere attempt to rewrite the life histories of *people they do not even know.*

As for the title of this section: long before I realized using logic is a fruitless endeavor when interacting with NRA's, I'd mentioned to one that I'd always disliked spinach. During my growing-up years, I only had one experience with the product: when it was served on a lunch tray in elementary school, I tried it and decided it tasted awful.

To the NRA population, though, there is no such thing as disliking something, objecting to something, not wanting to do something-- *it is all about your past.* And it is never about anything as trivial as disliking a specific food. In the hands of NRA's, it is about taking away your rights, taking away your free will. And if they cannot get under your skin and obtain cooperation from you directly, they will take their "game" to other people in or around your life.

When it comes to the bottom line of this topic, it should be as clear as the solution to 'Special Knowledge.' Whether an NRA is taking this approach to you or to someone else in your life, logic should be quite evident: they do not know you, they do not know your life history, and if they claim to have knowledge or information that you yourself do not have they are liars and manipulators. Not only are they dismissing the facts presented in modern science, they are dismissing their own programs for their own purposes.

"THOUGHT-STOPPING"

It was yet another topic I had never even heard of, much less witnessed or experienced, before I became involved with 12-Step programs. It did not come up in my ages-ago psychology classes, nor did it ever come up with the wide variety of people I'd known and interacted with in my life before the programs. While I did not notice whether the subject was addressed by the individual who made a long list of so-called "mind games" on a sheet of paper, it is a subject that should have been included, as it is extremely common in the programs.

For the longest time, with nothing else to go on, I simply thought the NRA's who engaged in this type of behavior were ignorant-- that regardless of their educational levels, they did not even know the true meanings and definitions of the words they used. I found this assumption was not accurate at all. This particular approach, known as *"thought-stopping,"* is intentional.

Thought-stopping involves using specific words that are intentionally chosen for their impact. The words are carefully and intentionally chosen for the purpose of obtaining a very strong and very negative reaction from the listener. The result of this process: the listener automatically focuses on his or her reaction, and it can interfere with the ability to think rationally.

One way to look at this issue: it's as if NRA's who take this approach use a thesaurus instead of a standard dictionary. What I mean by that is while dismissing the dictionary-definitions of words, it's as if they browse through synonyms and select the one that will have the most negative impact.

Naturally, as with anything pertaining to NRA's in 12-Step programs, it can get worse and weirder. If a person is subjected to this approach often enough, he or she may actually become *conditioned* to have a strong, negative reaction *any time* he or she hears those words or terms. Individuals who are otherwise rational may feel like Pavlov's dogs-- with conditioned reactions and responses.

The NRA who virtually dragged me to my first Narcotics Anonymous meeting was one example. As an NRA who had "double-digit" time in at least two 12-Step programs, it was as if she had her own personal repertoire of thought-stopping words and terms. The remarks she made about the elderly man *molesting* women was one example. Consider how an average person reacts, and what he or she thinks, when hearing this word and its variations.

A second example, used by that NRA and various others, was *torture.* Again, consider an average person's reaction to that word.

In both of these examples, she and other speakers were referring to situations in which "bother" or "annoy" would have been appropriate-- but "bother" and "annoy" do not produce the kinds of strong, negative reactions produced by "molested" and "tortured."

Another example she used was *rape.* She insisted anything that makes a person uncomfortable is 'sexual abuse,' but that it is not enough to call it 'sexual abuse,' it must be described as 'rape.' When I told her what the actual definition is of that particular word, she became huffy and said the dictionary is wrong. (If you are not yet aware of it, NRA's have the attitude that they and only they are right, and everyone and everything else is wrong).

Another thought-stopping word that is used with regularity amongst NRA's is *abuse.* While the American Psychiatric Association describes the word to mean using 'fear, humiliation, and verbal or physical assaults' to gain the upper-hand over others, NRA's do not go by these descriptions. Instead, they take the approach that anything they or someone else does not like is 'abuse.'

A common tactic amongst NRA's is to interrogate people about 'who *abused* you when you were a child?' This particular tactic is used in an attempt to cause people to distrust the individuals who had been in their early lives, to create discord, and to give the impression that no one outside *The Program* is, or ever was, trustworthy. After all, no one could trust someone who *abused* them.

It is also used to manipulate people's behaviors in the present. When a person is told everything he or she does or says is 'abusive,' you can end up with a person who is afraid to do or say *anything*.

'*Control*' is another common thought-stopper. Similar to these other words and terms, the way it is used amongst the NRA population bears no resemblance to its intended meaning. NRA's do not use the word to mean 'dominating' someone, or exerting 'undue influence' over another person; they use it to underline their antisocial belief that there should be no rules or laws in society, families, or life.

And, while it is a popular term in "pop-psych," research netted a source that went much further back than the "pop-psych" material that has been contaminating society for generations. The source: a well-known writer from the Beat Generation. This individual, who went through his life with heroin addiction and killed his own wife while under-the-influence, expressed his opinion that the United States government was a 'control machine,' and that one should not allow the government to 'control' them.

It is a classic NRA approach. Beginning with the approach that the government-- or one's family, or society in general-- must not tell you that you cannot use illegal drugs, NRA's eventually extend this approach to every subject in existence. And the approach that laws and rules do not apply to them is one of the most common 'symptoms' of sociopathy.

When we are discussing thought-stopping, there is an additional factor to consider. While all of the words and terms mentioned above, and many other words and terms, are a matter of normal vocabulary that is misused by NRA's, there are words and terms in an entirely different category. Some experts (as listed in *Quicksand*) refer to them as *buzzwords*.

The best way to explain buzzwords: while they are generally not a part of an average person's vocabulary, they are often used by NRA's to give the impression that they have knowledge. As the experts stated, buzzwords are often picked out of context from psychology books, mental health material, and other sources designed for education and professional use.

The catch, though: NRA's are not educated professionals. As one expert source stated, they are individuals who intentionally misuse words and terms for the purpose of 'controlling other people's behaviors.'

Although there is a wide variety of such terms, one you were likely to have heard in the programs is *"Codependent."* The term is often misused to mislead individuals into thinking there is something very, very wrong with them. However, if you take a look at the definitions of this term, you will realize 'codependent' is exactly what NRA's *want.* They do not want individuals who are self-assured, independent, or fully functioning. They want pigeons who "do not know who they really are- what they think, feel, believe, know, and want;" they want pigeons who "cannot think for themselves, cannot act without 'guidance,' and care more about what others think of them than what they think about themselves."

The most important point to keep in mind about thought-stopping: when you take a clear look at NRA's and their lives, it is not difficult to see how they use this tactic to "stack the odds in their favor." First, they use these words and terms to create negative reactions in other people. Second, and equally important, is they fail to acknowledge when these words and terms pertain to *themselves.*

Throughout my years of involvement with 12-Step programs, I encountered many, many examples. Although it should not be relevant, the NRA's who engaged in thought-stopping were all strangers-- individuals whom I did not even know. Using a term that came from one NRA, all of these individuals attempted to "impose their will" on me-- with everything from manipulations to flat-out threats, attempting to take over every aspect of my everyday life. Yet-- you would not hear a one of them admitting their behavior constituted *control and abuse.*

However, there is another point to consider. Regardless of one's opinion of 12-Step programs, the approach of thought-stopping is yet one more example of NRA's who have no interest in real recovery-- and do not even care what their own programs say. Start by thinking of the words and terms commonly used-- and misused-- by the NRA population. You will not find them in the 12-Step literature-- because none of it has anything to do with their 'programs.'

"THE MECHANICAL MAN (OR WOMAN)"

For a long time, I looked at the 12-Step programs as being like a secret club, where the only requirement for membership was to know the language. An additional approach, though, was if one does not know the language, all it means to NRA's is the person is simply 'not ready' to acknowledge or accept it. Looking back, there is one specific approach that covers it. You are likely to hear or experience it frequently within the programs.

It is sometimes described as *"act as if;"* and it is also described as *"fake it 'til you make it."* It can be seen as showing up regularly for 12-Step meetings when you do not belong in one, and it can be seen as expecting individuals to "parrot" phrases that the individuals either do not believe or even know to not be true. The purpose: if you continue this dishonesty long enough and/or often enough, you may start to believe it yourself.

Although there can be many different topics covered in 'act as if' and 'fake it 'til you make it,' the initial topic you are likely to encounter is alcoholism or drug addiction. And one of the creepiest parts of this approach is you will find it in 12-Step program members who are essentially honest and have no wrongful motives, as well as in the NRA population.

When you are in a 12-Step program meeting, you are expected to introduce yourself when it is your turn to speak. However, there is something else that is expected of you. It is not enough to say your name-- you are expected to also 'identify' yourself as an alcoholic or an addict. I think it is important to add this approach is used even in "open meetings," where anyone with any interest in the subject is said to be welcome.

Depending on whether or not you cooperate, you will receive either of two responses from others in the meeting. If you do not say "I am an alcoholic" or "I am an addict," the reactions from members will be negative. From smirks and snorting to 'know-all' glances, the reaction will be that you are simply too messed-up to realize you have a problem.

In contrast, making those statements will result in positive reactions-- whether the statements are true or not. You may see big wide smiles, heads nodding happily, or the "thumbs-up" sign. While a person in this position is being conditioned to say something about himself that may not even be true, this kind of positive reinforcement can further his belief that he should lie.

I became involved with 12-Step programs without any substance-abuse problems. Yet I encountered this approach time and time again, both from well-meaning members who appeared to believe everyone had the problems they had, and NRA's who had their own 'personal agendas.' In some instances, individuals had no idea whether or not I had substance-abuse problems, but in other instances individuals knew I did not but still expected me to lie.

I encountered this approach in other people, too. In a number of situations, there were individuals who were not alcoholics or drug addicts, yet were pressured to say they were. One young woman, for example, attended meetings to be supportive of her fiance, who was a recovering addict. One of the first things I noticed about her was she did not like to drink. Whenever her fiance would pour a drink for himself and one for her, she would take an obligatory sip and leave the rest. When the subject of drugs came up, I learned she was not a drug user. She had smoked marijuana a few times in the past, but didn't really like it. Yet, whenever it was her turn to speak in a meeting, she followed her name by saying "and I am *an addict.*"

Another woman showed up at a meeting, explaining "I don't think I'm an alcoholic- but my counselor says I am." While I was not yet familiar with the "trend" of drug and alcohol counselors being 12-Step program members themselves, I knew this specific counselor belonged to at least two 12-Step programs. And, as I later learned, addiction counselors often pressure individuals to join these programs whether they belong there or not. In addition, the counselor was dismissing what the original 12-Step program itself says on the subject: that no one but the alcoholic himself can 'diagnose' himself as an alcoholic.

These are only a couple of examples I encountered, as well as my own personal experiences. As for the latter, one incident comes to mind. One of the members, who did not have any wrongful motives, asked me to take the role of "moderator" in one of his meetings. When I politely refused, he politely chided me with "You're not showing Willingness." The fact is I was perfectly 'willing' to lead his meeting-- but I did not think I should be 'willing' to say "I am a drug addict" when I certainly was not.

I had similar experiences on other occasions. In meetings where very few people were present, I was often asked to "do the readings." This involved reading pages from 12-Step literature before the meetings began. And, naturally, anyone who did this was expected to add "I am an alcoholic" or "I am an addict." When there were more readings than people, it was between difficult and impossible to simply refuse to do it. The same issue came up in meetings I was asked to "chair," because the chairperson was not present.

What it comes down to is the 'act as if' approach is dishonest-- whether you are unsure of yourself or perfectly knowledgeable about the facts, you are expected to 'fake it 'til you make it.' And the bottom line is if you continue to 'fake it,' you may indeed 'make it' to the point that you fully believe you are exactly like them-- not only in terms of alcoholism or drug addiction, but the entire screwed-up way of life that goes along with it.

For NRA's, the goal of turning people into parrots is not about pressuring people to accept these things about themselves; it is not about getting individuals to acknowledge real problems so they can work toward effective solutions. Instead, it is about turning human beings into little more than robots, mechanically cooperating with whatever is expected of them.

COMPARING 12-STEP PROGRAMS TO DOMESTIC VIOLENCE

It must be clearly stated one does not have to be in an intimate relationship, or any kind of personal relationship, to have experiences in the 12-Step programs that are similar to domestic violence. Speaking from my own personal experiences, I encountered a number of these similarities in NRA's who were total strangers. The point: if you enter their 'world,' or even get too close to it, you may have a wide range of experiences that are common to battered women.

In domestic violence situations, batterers often isolate their victims. If you have the misfortune of meeting NRA's, you may find individuals who dictate who you will and will not associate with, who you can and cannot trust, where you will and will not go. If an NRA creates a 'hostage situation,' you may find everyone from your social network to your 'support' system is no longer in your everyday life. This can include close friends, family members, and other trustworthy people.

In domestic violence situations, batterers often dictate their victims' everyday lives. NRA's will tell you what clothing or styles to wear, what you must and cannot do with your time, and other factors that involve your daily life.

In domestic violence situations, batterers require their victims to 'answer to' them. NRA's will assert that everything from your thoughts and feelings to your behavior and actions are 'their business.' Nothing is *yours*-- nothing is personal or private.

In domestic violence situations, batterers "call the shots." NRA's take the approach that they have the upper-hand over you and others. You are expected to believe you no longer have the right to your personal choices and decisions-- that the NRA's will make your choices and decisions *for* you.

In domestic violence situations, batterers operate by intimidating their victims. NRA's are no different. Personally, I have experienced physical violence, threats of physical harm, and threats against members of my family. I have also experienced threats of homelessness- that I'd lose my apartments; threats that my pets would be killed; and threats that I'd be turned over to Social Services and the police for things I did not do, and mental health practitioners-- all if I did not cooperate with what NRA's wanted me to do. And there were even three NRA's who threatened my life. *'Recovery'? 'Sanity'? 'Working a program'? Only by the definitions of non-recovered alcoholics/addicts in 12-Step programs. And par for the course, each one of the NRA's who threatened my life had "double-digit clean/sober time" in their programs.*

In domestic violence situations, one of the most common tactics is attacking their victims' mental stability and credibility. NRA's have attacked everything from my general morality and fitness to my mental health. Similar to domestic violence situations, NRA's use this tactic to ensure no one will listen to you or believe you if you try to reach out for help. When abusers lie their asses off to portray you as mentally unstable and a horrible person, it is almost guaranteed that they will achieve their goal.

As I stated in *Quicksand,* there was virtually no experience I had during my 12-Step program involvement that other former members did not later echo from their own experiences. And these comparisons to domestic violence are not exceptions. *'We've got ya where we want ya- do what we say or else'* is a common theme amongst the NRA population everywhere.

What it comes down to are *behaviors that no reasonable person should ever be expected to tolerate.* While no person, regardless of age, gender, or personal situation, should ever be expected to tolerate *battering* from partners or anyone else in their personal lives, it "goes double" when referring to NRA's in 12-Step programs.

Yet these kinds of "horror stories" are far too common in the 12-Step programs. You may find anyone from "sponsors" and other oldtimers to general program members attempting to put you or someone else in the position of *victim.* And if you check some of today's most popular websites or written material that deals with this topic, you may see your own experiences addressed in what some call "the wheel of violence."

However, while many of us have been on the receiving-end of actual physical violence from NRA's, there is another important similarity between domestic violence situations and what you may encounter or experience in the 12-Step programs: there can be plenty of *violence* even if actual physical attacks do not occur. Isolation, threats against you or your family members, and all of the other examples described above are acts of *violence.*

And, unfortunately, there is another similarity: as anyone who is knowledgeable about domestic violence when it involves battered women, violence *can and will escalate.* In other words, if physical attacks have not yet occurred, it is in your best interest to realize they are likely to occur at some point. Because, as abusers delight in power, they want to weaken you further and further until there is virtually nothing left of you.

In fact, there have been a number of incidents where 'virtually' ceased to be accurate. There have been 12-Step program members who literally lost their lives to others in the programs. As evidence of this, there are family members who have filed "wrongful death" lawsuits against the 12-Step programs after their loved ones were murdered by other members of the programs. And while this is extreme enough for no sensible person to dismiss the violence in 12-Step programs, there have also been many members-- male and female, various age groups-- who were sexually assaulted and forcibly raped by their own 'sponsors' and other program members.

These issues are extreme enough and widespread enough that one of their "General Service Trustees" brought violence within the programs to their attention by way of an "internal memo." His request for these issues to be investigated and resolved was ignored.

So, widespread as it is, nothing is done about NRA's who are violent toward others. It does not only involve criminals who are 'sentenced' to 12-Step programs by the courts, but the majority of NRA's who were never reported. Whether an NRA whom you do not know attempts to present himself or herself as your "friend," attempts to strike up a personal relationship with you with or without your interest, or begins to weasel his or her way into your personal life or personal space, this is a topic you need to take seriously.

Again, none of these behaviors should be tolerated regardless of the source. If you think about women who are abused in their own homes, have no one to turn to and no way out, you have a clear view of what many of us have experienced in 12-Step programs-- not even by friends or partners, but often by total strangers who take one look at you and decide you are the perfect target.

All abusers need their victims to be weak, helpless and powerless, and vulnerable. If you are none of these things, these characteristics can be created by using the same methods and tactics used in domestic violence situations. And while battered women certainly do not deserve to be abused, neither do individuals who made the mistake of becoming involved with 12-Step programs.

An additional point to consider on this subject: it certainly shows that the NRA population is clueless about what constitutes 'recovery.' Or, as some say with sarcasm: "boy, he/she must have a *great program."*

And the bottom line: *abuse is abuse, and violence is violence,* whether it is a piece of worthless trash beating his wife or girlfriend, or whether these forms of abuse and violence come from NRA's you meet in a 12-Step program.

"YOUR 'PICKER' DOESN'T WORK"

The 12-Step program literature is very clear about the scope of a 12-Step program. The alleged purpose is to assist individuals in recovering from their addictions. With this in mind, the role and scope of all individuals in the programs is to 'share their strength, hope, and experience' of what worked for them in their own recovery processes.

I'm guessing there is not a one of us who separated ourselves from the programs who would not gag at that description of 12-Step programs and members. The reason: NRA's do not care what their own programs say. Instead, you will find NRA's-- from "sponsors" and other oldtimers to general members-- who not only claim special knowledge they do not have, but present themselves as "authority figures."

In doing so, they are essentially closing and throwing away their own 12-Step programs with the attitude they know "more, different, and better" than the programs they claim to follow. And whether they are trying to make themselves look or feel more important than they are, or attempting to gain power over other people, there is no aspect of your life they will not try to intrude into and take over.

The title of this section is a reference to experiences I have been told about by a number of former members. I had some, but little, experience with it myself. Specifically, the way it is approached: NRA's try to convince you that you do not have what it takes to select an "appropriate" partner, so they will do this *for* you.

One important point is all the individuals I heard from were adults. With years or decades of life experience, adults in various age groups were told they could not choose their own potential spouse or significant-other.

A second important point: NRA's who take this approach are often strangers. While the approach is offensive enough in general, it is crazier yet when people who do not even know you claim they are in a better position than you to make such a decision.

A third point: when it comes to NRA's, they are completely clueless about what constitutes a 'healthy' relationship. In fact, one NRA used that term to describe her relationship with her live-in boyfriend who was physically, sexually, and verbally abusive toward her.

So what you have in these situations is not a matter of "the blind leading the blind." It is often a matter of 'the blind' attempting to lead someone who is not.

Personally, I had a couple of experiences with 12-Step program members who urged me to comply with their views of what relationships consist of and who should and should not be in relationships. While everyone is entitled to his own opinion, pressuring others to comply with their viewpoints is not ok. In another instance, an NRA pressured me to give up a friend because she did not like the person.

There is nothing in your personal life that is within the scope of 12-Step programs-- and this is certainly the case when it comes to choosing someone to be *in* your life. It does, though, show there are no limits to what NRA's will go to when they wish to have power over other people.

You may not understand how extreme this is if you have not experienced it yourself. However, you can clarify it by thinking about someone in your life. Whether the person is a friend, coworker, or a member of your own family, what do you think the person's reaction would be if you were to approach him and tell him "Your 'picker' doesn't work- so I will select your spouse or partner for you"? The person is likely to deem you an arrogant, intrusive asshole-- and may even say so. And he would be right.

Within the programs, though, there is a connected factor. While it would obviously be arrogant and intrusive to take this approach to a friend, coworker, or family member, NRA's are not in any of these categories. They are nothing more than alcoholics or drug addicts whom you have met in a 12-Step meeting. If you would not take "advice" about your personal life from a stranger who approached you in a grocery store, there is even less sense in taking such 'advice' from program members who are drowning in years or decades of their own messed-up life histories.

A huge problem with the NRA population is they prefer to focus on "others," rather than on themselves. They enjoy feeling more important than they are, having the upper-hand and control over other people, and claiming credit where it is not due. At the top of the list, NRA's love *orchestrating* other people's lives-- if you fall into this trap, you may become nothing more than a pawn on a chessboard or a puppet bouncing at the end of an NRA's puppet strings.

If you must interact with NRA's, develop the habit of stating *"My personal life is none of your business."* Do not be surprised if you are then accused of 'not being honest' or 'not working your program.' While your personal life has nothing to do with either of these issues, they are two of the most common approaches NRA's use to get into other people's lives and obtain cooperation.

Perhaps you did not make the best 'choices' or 'decisions' in the past. If not, it is up to you to examine and resolve them, and move on to better choices and decisions. But it is *not* the place of NRA's to assert that they know your personal life better than you do, and attempt to take it over. It is neither the scope of a so-called 'recovery program,' nor the role of anyone in it, to take this approach to any program member or anyone else in general. And if they do, it is a good idea to question their motives-- and get them out of your life as quickly as possible.

"PRAY FOR THEM- THEY ARE 'SPIRITUALLY SICK'"

"Praying for others," "accepting others"-- in the real world, these approaches can benefit everyone concerned. However, there can be many situations within the 12-Step programs where you should never even consider taking these approaches.

If you wish to retain your peace of mind, safety, and sanity, eliminate these program concepts from your vocabulary-- or at least reserve them for people who deserve it. And, if you have been involved with 12-Step programs, you should have come to the realization that all people are not equally deserving-- and some, in fact, do not deserve it at all.

If you have read *Quicksand,* you have seen many examples of the latter. You can probably think of many examples from your own 12-Step program experiences, too. One of the first examples I encountered is described in the first section of *Quicksand.* Feel free to repeat after me: "Individuals who took away the life of a small child and then covered up the crime *do not deserve 'acceptance'.*" Furthering the sheer lunacy of the 12-Step program concept, the individual asserted that *no one can judge him.* Repeat after me: *"Yes, we can."*

Think about it from a logical, non-program point of view. Human beings make mistakes, and occasionally serious mistakes. However, it is what they do about it afterward that makes a difference. One of the most warped things I found in the 12-Step programs is NRA's who made mistakes-- regardless of how large or small-- believe belonging to a 12-Step program absolves them of any and all responsibility for anything they have done in the past, and anything they may do in the future.

The first point to keep in mind: depending on the circumstances, anger, outrage, or a variety of other responses, are natural, normal, healthy reactions to horrible behaviors. When NRA's claim you cannot or should not have these reactions, they are trying to shut you down and shut you up.

A second point: think of what is commonly known as "jailhouse converts," and it is quite similar to NRA's in 12-Step programs. You may have heard of various criminals who "found God" or "found Jesus" when they were incarcerated for cold-blooded murder or other horrible crimes-against-persons. The catch: you can bet your boots the largest percentage of these individuals are *phonies.* If you read about their actions after they "find God," "find Jesus," or "get 'saved'," you see most have the approach common to sociopaths: WIIFM (What's In It For Me). You will not find many whose "newfound status" consists of a genuine love for the Lord, the intention to follow the ways of their 'higher power,' or to do good for others without gaining something for themselves.

Throughout my years of involvement with 12-Step programs, I knew many NRA's who took exactly the same approach: 'What's in it for me?' Similar to jailhouse converts, they glom onto a label they feel will benefit them in some way.

The majority of these phonies chose the term 'christian.' It did not take much effort to see they did not equate the term to "what would Jesus do?" I cannot recall a single self-professed 'christian' in 12-Step programs who was in any way following the teachings of Jesus Christ. Instead, there were NRA's who used the term in an attempt to place themselves above others, to claim being 'saved' meant they were not accountable for their immoral or criminal behaviors, and even one who stated he 'got saved' because he 'believed it would help him get more women.'

NRA's who claim different belief-systems were no different and no better. From "Native American spirituality" to "Wicca," they claimed beliefs they did not follow. From basic moral codes to how they treated others, it was all a matter of picking what was convenient from their "religions" and dismissing everything else.

Where does this leave the rest of us who either witnessed or experienced horrible behaviors by NRA's? Whether they are 'spiritually sick' or not, it is not up to us to 'pray for' them, 'accept' them, or believe we cannot 'judge' them. Whether their lousy behaviors affected us or someone else, we need to take back our human prerogative to say wrong is wrong, and that they cannot rely on us to be their "covers." If they claim we 'cannot judge' them because we are not God, then perhaps they should look to God for 'forgiveness.' The catch, though, is NRA's do not believe they have done anything wrong-- they merely use religion and the programs as an excuse.

If all of this does not show NRA hypocrisy clearly enough, all we need to do is look at what the original 12-Step book has to say about injustice and anger, and then recall there was probably not a one of us who ever heard this viewpoint during our involvements with the programs.

First, perhaps we can look at the purported author of that particular book as the original NRA, who claimed a person who is wronged has no more business being angry about the behavior than the individual who wronged him. However, he went on to state that anger is extremely dangerous to alcoholics (and would probably have included drug addicts, too, if the subject had been addressed in the book) because the strong, negative feeling could lead the person to relapse.

However, while individuals in the 12-Step programs asserted this to be true, neither I nor any other former members I have known ever heard this approach used within the programs. Instead, NRA's presented a variety of other, totally outrageous, 'reasons' why anger is never an acceptable response or reaction to anything. Ranging from "anger is not spiritual" to "anger is a sign of mental health problems," NRA's take this approach to shut people *down* and shut people *up*.

Now, back in the real world, you may still be under the influence of these approaches. There is an accurate, sensible, healthy way to look at the subject. Similar to all other normal human emotions, the ability to feel and express anger is part of being human. In addition, while "appropriate" is a concept NRA's cannot grasp regardless of the subject, there are both appropriate and inappropriate ways of expressing anger. A minor incident should not provoke uncontrollable rage, and unless you or someone else is actually in danger anger can be expressed without harming anyone.

The main point, though, is coming out from under the influence of the NRA population includes the ability to fully feel and appropriately express all human emotions-- including anger. You are not expected to brush off wrongs intentionally committed against you, or stand by when you know someone else is being wronged. In the real world, "acceptance" and "pray for them- they are spiritually sick" are not appropriate responses to crimes-against-persons, and violations of other people's rights.

Who exactly benefits from this NRA approach? If you think clearly, you will see no one but the NRA's benefit. They are off the hook for whatever they have done, and it is virtually an open door to continue behaviors that harm others.

Whether behavior consists of an isolated incident or an ongoing stream of incidents, it must be kept in context. One mistake does not make a lifestyle-- unless the individual chooses to make it a way of life. Wrongful behaviors are not all alike-- obviously, there are huge differences between minor annoyances and crimes that injure others or take their lives. There are individuals who do wrong, intentionally or unintentionally, and have a solid enough conscience that they genuinely try to set things right. And there are NRA's-- many of whom meet the definition of *sociopaths*. If you take the approach "pray for them" or "we cannot judge and must accept them," you are both weakening yourself and others who are in their paths.

Sociopaths do not believe right vs. wrong applies to them. They believe people who have consciences are fools. They believe genuine concern for other people, following legitimate laws and rules, and all of the other aspects that make the rest of us human beings are nothing but signs of weakness.

Bearing this in mind, NRA's in this category *do not deserve* our "acceptance," our "friendship," or the approach that they cannot be judged for the things they have done and the things they do. And whether or not they are 'spiritually sick,' we should not fall into the trap of believing we must intervene with prayers and dismiss the harm they have caused to others. Like jailhouse converts, they can take their phoniness to their 'higher powers' and leave the rest of us out of it.

As for us, though, anger and appropriate expressions of anger are not only within our rights as human beings, but show that we *are* human beings. Do not allow NRA's in 12-Step programs to take that away from you-- and if they already have, begin to reclaim it. Do it now.

"ANONYMITY BE DAMNED"

Let me be clear: I am by no means suggesting anyone who has freed himself or herself from a 12-Step program resort to the underhanded tactics often used by NRA's. In fact, this topic is one of the many that shows NRA's care nothing about what their own programs teach, including the basic principles.

Regardless of the particular program you were involved in, its name contained the word *"Anonymous."* This word is used to highlight the importance of personal privacy-- both in terms of who belongs to 12-Step programs and information members share with their groups, sponsors, or other members.

If you are like most of us, you have known many NRA's who do not abide by what their own programs teach. You may have found NRA's who inform others of who attends 12-Step meetings, or who has stated he or she is an alcoholic or a drug addict. You may have found NRA's who pass other people's personal and confidential information around for gossip, power, or manipulation. We can take these intentional wrongs as a clear sign that NRA's are only interested in personal gain-- and refuse to stoop to the same low behavior.

However, "anonymity" does not cover criminal behavior or behaviors that harm others. One of the most serious mistakes one can make is to believe in the approach "Whatever goes on within the program must stay within the program." If you are like most people who have separated themselves from 12-Step programs, you have had one or more experiences with this mistake. In other words, while the programs advise that any and all wrongful behaviors committed by program members should be addressed to one's 'sponsor,' one's 'group,' or one's 'local group,' you may have experienced the results of this approach.

Whether the programs are trying to absolve themselves of any responsibility, or whether they are operating with blinders on and actually believe this approach can resolve problems, this is not the issue. The issue is this approach does not work, and can even make matters worse. You are not likely to find an 'offender' removed from a group, or in any way held accountable for his actions.

One one side of the issue, you may find you are up against nothing more nor less than a social network. On the other side, 'sponsors,' groups, and local groups do not have a professional capacity-- nor are they intended to. This is why criminal behavior and other wrongs against members must be addressed to the proper authorities. As the books state, no one in a 12-Step program is a counselor, social worker, law enforcement official, or any other type of authority figure. So if someone commits a crime against you or someone else, choose the most appropriate authority-- *not* members of the 12-Step program.

If this issue has not affected you directly, you can be sure it has affected at least one person you know. In fact, it was addressed to the main offices of a 12-Step program by an individual on their board who realized exactly how serious and widespread the issue is within the 12-Step programs. While the main offices ignored his request to take steps to deal with the issue, the memo was "leaked" for everyone to see. In part, it reads:

"Complaints have been received about groups of members and individual members who are involved in the following behaviors toward other members and groups in the fellowship:

Actual or implied violence;
Bullying;
Intimidation;
Stalking;
Threatening behavior;
Verbal, emotional, and sexual abuse.
There is confusion about taking legal action against perpetrators because the victims think they will be breaking anonymity, fear retribution, and that they won't be believed."

In contrast, we can look at how the two most well-known 12-Step programs advise people to deal with these and other 'behaviors' when they occur within the 12-Step program. I received two personal replies from the main offices of these programs.

The reply from one main office included this advice:

"It is indeed regrettable that members of AA are amongst those who act inappropriately toward others... good sponsorship is the key to helping the newcomer avoid such pitfalls...

"Clearly, there are times within AA that the newcomer or any other member may face the kinds of difficulties and abuses that are encountered in life in general, and good sponsorship helps in resolving these and other problems appropriately."

The reply I received from the other 12-Step program main office was not much different:

"Grievances with individual members or trusted servants should be addressed with the group or service committee where the issues are taking place."

However, they did include an additional bit of advice one is not likely to hear anywhere else within the programs or from program members:

"If there are crimes being committed, the proper place to address that matter would be with the appropriate legal authorities."

And this latter bit of advice says it all. If an NRA's behavior involves criminal actions toward you or someone else, do not be conned or bullied into believing you must tolerate it, and do not be conned or bullied into believing 12-Step program members can effectively deal with the problem-- or that they would even want to.

Speaking from my own experiences, I met very few members of 12-Step programs who had any concern about what 'others' go through, or their fates. I was, and continue to be, very grateful to the few who were in this category. They showed themselves as compassionate human beings, people who knew the difference between right and wrong, and had the courage to offer assistance.

Unfortunately, such human beings were in the minority. But while 'sponsors,' 'groups,' and 'service committees' refused to do anything on behalf of individuals who were wronged or harmed, there was yet another approach that caused my skin to crawl. Amongst NRA's in the 12-Step programs-- those who meet the programs' definition of "oldtimers"-- so-called 'help' was offered, but at a price. I actually had a number of much older individuals with "double-digit clean/sober time," offering their assistance in various situations if I would provide sex in return. And upon finding I was not a prostitute, they brushed off my situations and did nothing.

An additional point that bears noting: neither of these main offices addressed the issue that wrongs are often committed *by* so-called sponsors and/or members of service committees. As only one example, I have heard from a number of people who reported that they and others were raped, sexually assaulted, stolen from, and a variety of other wrongs, *by their own sponsors.* This includes, but is not limited to, teenagers in the 12-Step programs who have been sexually assaulted by their much-older 'sponsors.' And as for 'service committees,' what is a person expected to do if the NRA's in question are members of those committees?

The answer: while it appeared to be an afterthought, the advice to take criminal behavior to 'the appropriate legal authorities' is the only sensible and appropriate course of action. Not only do members of 12-Step programs have no authority to deal with serious issues, in most cases they simply do not care. As only one bit of evidence: the numbers of individuals who, after being victimized by crimes, are told to "look for *their part*" in the crimes, as if they themselves are responsible for what happened to them. Some of the stories I have been told are enough to make your blood crawl: from having the misfortune of meeting or trusting the wrong kind of person, to being in the wrong place at the wrong time, they attempt to justify criminal behavior and blame the victims.

"What's say" we refuse to tolerate this any longer. If you or someone you know has been the victim of a crime at the hands of a 12-Step program member, don't waste your time with 'sponsors,' 'the group,' or your local 'service committee.' Instead, get in touch with the appropriate legal authorities. And whether you have experienced or witnessed criminal behavior within the programs or not, take every opportunity to warn others about these issues.

Keep in mind they are not 'program issues,' they are issues of human rights-- the right of every person to have safety and personal dignity. We are, indeed, our brothers' (and sisters') 'keepers'.

DIFFERENT PEOPLE, DIFFERENT ADVICE

Frankly, it did not even occur to me at the time. In a number of situations, advice I was given (whether I asked for any or not) depended on whether the individuals in question were or were not members of 12-Step programs. In retrospect, individuals who had nothing to do with 12-Step programs had sound advice based on common sense, while program members offered lousy advice that was in no one's best interest but "furthered the cause" of *The Program*. (On a side note: in retrospect, I also see 12-Step program members are those who generally "offer advice" when one does not ask for it).

You can start by looking at any topic that is relevant to you or your life. Not only are non-members more likely to have a common sense approach, they are more likely to know you, care about you, and consider the eventual outcome of the advice they offer. In contrast, none of these points are accurate when we are referring to members of 12-Step programs. They are not your friends, not your family, and lack both common sense and concern for the consequences. Although you will find many who offer advice solely to make themselves look or feel important, it is the *Program* approach you need to be concerned about.

I can start with some of my own experiences. First, there was one particular situation that played itself out over a relatively long period of time, and in a variety of locations. Unfortunately, while I was not completely brainwashed by 12-Step programs, I did make the mistake of believing that one *should and must* follow the advice of program members-- even when it is in direct opposition to one's own good judgment, and even when it is in direct opposition to advice from true friends and family members.

In other words, while I never fell into the 12-Step program brainwashing trap of "let the program do your thinking for you," I was dangerously close to that trap when I dismissed my own good judgment and the good judgment of people who had legitimate places in my life in favor of doing what program members said I should do.

This particular situation involved an NRA who differed from the other NRA's I met throughout the years. Unlike the other NRA's, he was not an 'oldtimer,' and lacked the many years of 12-Step program experience the other NRA's often used to manipulate other people. Instead, he lied to get what he wanted, told "sob-stories" to get what he wanted, and fully believed everyone was responsible for him but himself. It was never a matter of "helping someone who needed help," but there were many people he managed to con. Not only did this include myself and a wide range of churches in at least three different states, but also 12-Step program members who did not know him well or did not know him at all. And it was individuals in the latter category who, upon being completely snowed by this NRA, offered advice that turned out to be quite destructive.

One member, for example, was on the receiving-end of long phone calls from the NRA. Although she had "double-digit clean/sober time" in the programs, she was unable to recognize his cons for what they were. Based on nothing more than what he said during their conversations, she bubbled about what a great person he was-- truly concerned about himself, others, and especially *'his program.' "He's doing the best he can!"* she exclaimed. Although I never had the opportunity to ask, I wondered if she still felt that way after he managed to bilk her out of hundreds of dollars that he never had any intention of repaying.

And this member was not unique. There were numerous others whom he took advantage of-- never in terms of genuinely needing 'help,' but with the approach that everyone was obligated to 'do for' him. But while conning people out of their hard-earned money was bad enough, it did not stop at that. While he looked at others as his source for short-term cash needs, he also looked at them as a way to pressure *me* into being his ongoing, longterm source of financial support. The result: all of these people insisted for me to continue 'helping' him was 'the right thing' to do.

(On a side note, there was something I did not think of until I was mapping out the material for this section. The way this NRA conned others into pressuring me to do what he wanted was also not unique. Each time he succeeded, he smirked behind their backs about what fools they were to believe everything he said. Remarking there was nothing I could do about it because none of them would care what I said, was quite similar to what I encountered at a later date from other NRA's-- asserting the individuals they conned with their lies would not believe me if I approached them and told them the truth. So it shows there are many similarities between NRA's who are little more than newcomers and NRA's who have been in their programs for years or decades.)

The consequences of this particular NRA and his tactics were extreme. However, none of the members he conned looked at any of the consequences, either longterm or short-term. As an example, after the NRA pilfered rent and household money to "treat" some of his street friends to a few days of drinking in a motel, virtually crawling to me for 'help' afterward, program members who should have been able to see him and the situation as they really were insisted he was 'so sorry' for his behavior and pressured me to provide shelter and support for him.

In this and other situations, the point is the 12-Step program population "sticks to their own kind." They believe no consequences are too extreme when it comes to expecting others to tolerate the outrageous behaviors of someone else who is "in a program." And what it comes down to is NRA's even use other members of their own programs to get their own way, no different than using people who are not in programs in order to get their own way. This example was only one of the many examples of how NRA's con *everyone* into believing they are good people with good intentions, and use that con to apply pressure to others.

Unfortunately, it is a lose/lose, "damned if you do and damned if you don't" scenario. On one side, whether you have one or a number of 12-Step program members ganging up on you, these individuals who have no concern for you personally also have no concern for the "wreckage" you will have to cope with if you follow their recommendations. On the other side, if you do not do what they 'advise' you to do, the results can range from labeling you a horrible person to actual threats. And if you have read *Quicksand,* you can recall a variety of situations in which I had 12-Step program members on one side and concerned individuals on the other. But whether the concerned individuals were true friends, members of my own family, or even the authorities, the members applied strong pressure to dismiss anything and everything these other people said, and do what *they* said instead.

If, like most 12-Step program members, you have been indoctrinated, brainwashed, cautioned, or pressured to not rely on your own good judgment and not request nor listen to advice and opinions from other people in your life, keep in mind a more relevant caution: NRA's who take this approach do not know you, and do not have your best interests in mind. While other people in your life may want you to be happy, healthy, and safe, this is not where NRA's are coming from. Whether they are completely conned by an NRA who wants something from you, enjoy orchestrating other people's lives, or believe it is "all about *The Program,"* they are not the people to listen to in any situation.

Instead, you are capable of applying your own good judgment and common sense to nearly any situation that occurs. And if you doubt this, or truly need advice, talk to someone whose opinion counts and is likely to have your best interests in mind. From longtime friends to family members, these individuals have a stake in your best interests-- NRA's in 12-Step programs do not.

Think about it very carefully: do you really believe individuals you barely know can know "more and better" about you and your life than longtime friends and members of your own family? Or that they have the kind of stake in the eventual outcome of any situation you may be in to make heeding their advice or opinions in any way sensible?

NRA's-- non-recovered addicts/alcoholics in 12-Step programs-- are either out for something themselves, or backing up someone who is. It is all about *The Program-- their own versions* of the program-- without any concern for the casualties and wreckage caused by their misguided "advice." And while the situation I described was only one of the numerous situations covered in this topic, the consequences included a temporary breakup of my own family, financial difficulties, interference with my educational plans, and tolerating both the presence and consistent chaos caused by the NRA in question.

And, as was the case with any situation that involved interference by 12-Step program members, none of it would have occurred had I simply followed my own common sense or listened to longtime friends and family members instead of caving in to pressure by 12-Step program members.

SURVIVAL

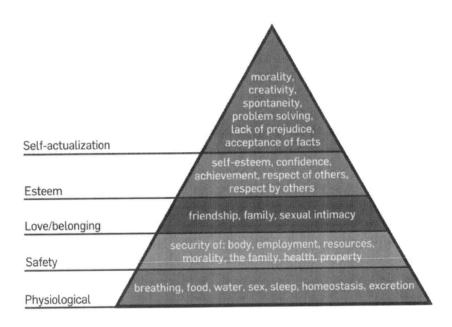

(as designed by Abraham Maslow)

    Survival is not living. It is barely existing. Speaking from my own experiences, which you may or may not be able to relate to, there were three very distinct categories. The categories included general chaos, the state of being on-edge, and situations in which I was actually in danger. How this is related to

Maslow's *Hierarchy of Needs:* the first two categories resulted in these levels crumbling and shattering, while the third category resulted in the basic needs levels being torn out from under me and everything above them collapsing. And when all of these levels are not left intact, there is virtually nothing left but the focus on Survival-- and the focus on survival is nothing but an animal instinct.

When we are talking about NRA's, there are two factors: their longterm alcohol or drug abuse, and the lifestyle that generally accompanies it. And to one degree or another, your *Hierarchy of Needs* will be influenced and affected if you have NRA's in or around your life. Your physical health will suffer, and your nerves will be shot. Whether you are a former member of 12-Step programs who is trying to deal with your own recovery, or someone who never had recovery issues at all, regaining your own life means understanding and dealing with these effects.

As one example of this topic: many years ago, it was extreme enough that I sought advice from both a health clinic and a priest. I should not have been surprised to find both offered the same opinions and the same advice, although their approaches and terminology differed. At the clinic, I was told the effects of trying to function in the midst of NRA's could kill me if I did not get out of that environment. The priest, straightforward as he was, said it was like 'living in a mental institution,' and remarked NRA's 'belong in an institution.' The bottom line: the human mind is not designed to cope with constant chaos.

At the time, I also managed to acquire a paperback book which, unfortunately, I have not been able to locate since. Its author, a psychologist, presented some common reasons some individuals not only make chaos a way of life, but actually believe it is normal. Two of the most common causes are living in dysfunctional families during one's early years, and parents or other adults who are neglectful. The catch, though, is to not waste your time and energy on trying to figure out why they are the way they are, but to eliminate their effects on *you.*

If you have NRA's in or around your life, you are expected to keep up with their chaos. As is the case with anything pertaining to the NRA population, they believe they are right and everyone else is wrong. It is especially a problem in environments where chaotic lifestyles are common. You may need to "buck the trend" in order to regain your life and your health.

If you have any doubts, ask yourself how many 12-Step program members you have known who did not claim to have some kind of mental health issues. While I have heard some claim schizophrenia and post-traumatic stress disorder, the most common condition claimed by NRA's is bipolar conditions. And although it is unlikely for individuals to go through years or decades of substance abuse without any consequences to their mental health, lifestyle factors can stand in the way of real recovery.

A few years ago, I discussed this topic with a longtime friend. She had been a psychiatric nurse for many decades, and took continuing-education classes throughout her career. It was quite interesting to find my viewpoint verified by a longtime professional. Stating bipolar conditions can be the result of genetic or organic causes, she said in most cases they are not-- in most cases, these 'bipolar' conditions are nothing more nor less than the effects of the environment and its lifestyle factors.

So on one side you have NRA's who never learned how to live healthy lives. They "run around like chickens with their heads cut off," never knowing what they are doing from one minute to the next. Concepts such as making plans, carefully considering options, and even basic daily routines are entirely foreign to them.

On the other side, they keep non-NRA's on edge because we never know when something will happen or how destructive it may be.

However, while these issues are serious enough and can be harmful enough to non-NRA's, you may also have encountered situations where you were actually in danger, in harm's way, or in the position of fighting for your life when fighting was not even an option.

And what all of these issues have in common is they reduce the rest of us to the level of basic survival. As a human being, you deserve more and better than this. And whether their destructive ways are used intentionally to harm others, or are nothing more than their own way of living, your freedom, health, and safety depend on freeing yourself from such influences.

Get NRA's out of your life, and begin to reclaim your own. If you have learned destructive lifestyle habits during your time in a program, or whether they were part of your life before you became involved with a program, now is the time to make changes. Not only do destructive individuals have to "go," so do unhealthy lifestyle factors. Neither spinning in a fog of chaos nor existing in fear need to sum up your life. You are not an animal who should spend your life with nothing more than survival instincts. All of those levels can be yours-- when you start to make changes.

"THERE'S SOMETHING ROTTEN- AND IT 'AIN'T' IN DENMARK"

One useful caution presented in a 12-Step book is "paralysis by analysis." The way we can look at this as pertaining to deprogramming: there is nothing to be gained, and precious time and effort to be lost, if you attempt to analyze, understand, or label NRA's. Many are indeed sociopaths, whether or not they are 'spiritually sick.' However, when your goal is deprogramming and recovering from 12-Step programs, a wiser way to look at it is *some people are just rotten to the core.*

You cannot "fix" them, you cannot "change" them. But you can start putting your own life back in order by seeing them for what they are. As a friend who is a minister said: "You will know them by their fruits"-- regardless of how long an NRA has been in a 12-Step program, how is he living his everyday life *today,* especially in terms of how he relates to or interacts with other people?

In *Quicksand,* you read about some 'doozies'-- not only from my experiences, but the experiences of numerous others who separated themselves from the programs. For the sake of clarity, though, I will add a few more experiences that pertain to this topic. It will show that some individuals, if they 'change' at all, change for the worst-- they are just rotten to the core.

First, there can be many ways NRA's get others to "do their bidding." If you have had the misfortune of tangling with an NRA, you may have noticed it was never about that one individual. NRA's have backup-- sometimes from the most unlikely sources. Naïve individuals may back up NRA's because they are conned into believing the NRA's are doing the right thing; in other instances, NRA's bribe, pay off, or threaten others into doing what they want. But while these issues are well known, one particular situation was entirely different. It was nothing more nor less than one screwed-up individual wanting to "please *Sponsor,*" and was willing to go to any extremes to do it.

This creep was approximately fifty years of age; and after he had destroyed his family and his life with drug and alcohol abuse, had been a longtime member of 12-Step programs. With an oppressive mother on one side and a bully for a sponsor on the other, it seemed he was quite familiar with following orders. As is common in the 12-Step programs, "Sponsor" was looked at as an authority figure, although he was nothing but a violent, hardened ex-con.

To please his sponsor, the creep agreed to commit some crimes against individuals the sponsor did not like. While neither of the individuals had done anything to deserve either the sponsor's wrath or the creep's participation, the creep stole a large amount of personal property from one individual, and told the sponsor he would commit multiple rapes against the second individual.

Within the programs, there are individuals like him who are perfectly willing to destroy innocent people on behalf of "Sponsor" or another member. And similar destruction can occur when individuals who are not even in 12-Step programs are sucked into it.

A second example was one I witnessed many years ago, but should by no means be considered an isolated incident. It shows anyone can be harmed by individuals who do not take 'recovery' seriously-- including children.

This particular incident involved a girl who was eleven or twelve years of age. All the little girl had done was go to the nearby park to play with a friend without first obtaining permission. But while her behavior may have been wrong, the reaction I witnessed from her father was extreme, out of line, and downright abusive. In front of me and others standing nearby, he hollered at her: *"I should tear up your ass right here!"*

My first thought was "What kind of monster talks to a child like that, and treats a child like that?!" but my thought was soon followed by "If this is the way he treats the child in public, in front of strangers, how much worse does he treat her in their own home?!"

This incident also showed the outrageous behaviors of NRA's-- including child abuse-- are by no means limited to alcoholics/addicts in the lower classes. While I did not know what the child's father did for a living, I was aware her mother was an attorney. So when it comes to NRA's, such factors as income level and employment are not relevant. *Some people are just rotten to the core.*

So once you have processed this information, what is the next- no pun intended- step? A wise approach is to simply decide they are not the kind of individuals you want in your life. If someone is being harmed, by all means contact the appropriate authorities. Otherwise, realize NRA's no longer have a place in your life, and most likely never did.

AFTERMATH

When freeing oneself from 12-Step programs, the approach may be *"Where do we go from here?"* If you are like most of us, there is plenty of wreckage and destruction to deal with, in addition to planning a new course of life. There are a couple of other points, though, that must be kept in mind.

First, freeing oneself from the programs means using every opportunity to reclaim *"Normal."* Regardless of what that term means to you, you can start by balancing it against the 12-Step programs. While you are no longer obligated to participate in their craziness, there is another factor that is more important: you are no longer in the position of "putting your seal-of-approval" on it. In other words, you no longer need to *act as if* it is all o.k. You no longer have to "call good evil, and evil good."

Second, if NRA's have been a part of your life for a period of time, changes will occur. From my experiences, both during and after the programs, NRA's fall into three distinct categories.

One category includes those who "vanish into thin air-never to be seen or heard from again." From my experiences, this represents the largest percentage of the NRA population. Whether they are individuals with whom you were on good terms, had difficulties, or barely knew, they take the approach *"You're not in the program anymore- so you are no longer our friend."* The point to bear in mind is individuals who take this approach *never were* your friends.

A second category includes those who take a *"Poor poor pitiful You"* approach. They assume you will *fail,* and many will even want you to fail. As one example: an oldtimer brushed off someone he had associated with for a long time with a shrug: *"He don't want what we got."* Such individuals will either try to drag you back to *The Program*-- or dismiss you as "hopeless and lost."

There is a third category. As you may recall from countless examples throughout *Quicksand,* they are what one expert in the field of pathology describes as *Cluster B Personality Disorders.* You may be familiar with the terms *sociopaths, psychopaths, antisocial personality, pathologicals.* And as the expert cautioned, these individuals who take human beings and human lives as nothing but "a game to win" do not disappear as easily as the others.

The expert states a wide variety of behaviors such individuals will continue to engage in, regardless of how much you want to be rid of them. Some of the examples the expert provided: they may continue to stalk you, harass you, turn other people against you, make up unfounded allegations against you, "stir up the pot," lie to the authorities, pay off other people to lie for them, continue to gaslight you or other people, make other people dread you or your situation, and various other behaviors to show they have power and control.

"DON'T DRIVE YOURSELF BATS"

You may have a variety of negative thoughts and feelings toward yourself regarding your involvement in 12-Step programs, or with the NRA population. If you have separated yourself from the programs, you now have the opportunity to make better choices-- ones that are in your own best interest, and the best interest of the people in your life.

Above all, there is something very important you can learn from the NRA population: a mistake does not make a lifestyle... it only does for those who have chosen to do it that way.

While I do not claim to be an expert on deprogramming, there is one approach I believe can be especially useful.

First, if you have participated in a 12-Step program, you probably obtained that program's main text book, and perhaps the volumes that accompanied it. Second, if you participated in a 12-Step program, you probably heard or read references to "approved program literature." Whether you currently own the books or read them online, there is something that requires great emphasis: most of the garbage you heard from NRA's *is not in those books.*

Next, some of what you heard from NRA's *can* be found in the literature-- but not in the form it was presented to you. This is where prooftexting and twisting what is written comes into the picture. You may have heard *"the book says..."* but if you take a closer look, that's not what it is talking about at all.

Next, consider how many NRA's present themselves as knowledgeable and authorities on any given subject-- and note what the literature says about *that.*

What all of these points come to: it shows a very clear distinction between individuals who are working toward recovery and the non-recovered alcoholic/addict population who become involved in 12-Step programs for very different reasons.

There are three important points to keep clearly in mind.

First, NRA's-- non-recovered alcoholics/addicts-- are almost never the way they present themselves; Second, any situation involving NRA's is never the way they present it; and third, when anything goes wrong or you assert yourself, it is always 'your fault.'

Although there are countless examples of these points throughout *Quicksand,* I will add another example for this little book. It clearly shows how all of these points are relevant in any situation that involves NRA's, and it is only one of many examples.

On a number of occasions, I was approached by an NRA who handed me little slips of paper on which he had printed his name and telephone number. Initially, I did not think it too odd, as I had seen him do the same with other people, explaining he had more space than he needed in his place and was looking for people who needed a place to rent. As desperate situations often lead to mistakes, I made the mistake of falling for this so-called offer.

The NRA took my mistake as the opportunity he was hoping for. Not only did he steal a large amount of personal property, I listened to a phone conversation in which he was telling another NRA that he would commit multiple acts of violence against me. Naturally, these incidents were enough for me to find different accommodations.

After doing so, I foolishly returned to the residence to retrieve whatever property was still there. By 'foolishly,' I mean I went by myself and approached the residence alone. However, when I called through the closed door that I'd come to get the items that belonged to my family members and myself, he called back at me through the closed door: *"You sick bitch- you belong here with me!"*

While I ended up needing assistance from a sheriff's deputy to retrieve our property, that in itself was not the main issue. The issue was how NRA's are not what they present themselves to be, situations are not as they present them, and the way they react if you assert your rights.

RIP VAN WINKLE

You may be familiar with the story of the person who fell asleep and did not awaken until twenty years later. Everything was different; people had changed, and many were deceased. Depending on how long you were involved with the programs, this is the way you may feel.

Repair and restore what you can, but it is also time to move forward. While you cannot recapture the years or decades the programs stole from your life, you can make the conscious decision to not allow them to take any more away from you.

WHAT SHOULD YOU DO?

Deprogramming is an essential part of reclaiming your own life. You can move ahead without the ever-present influence of 12-Step programs. Regardless of what you want the rest of your life to be like, you can be free to pursue your dreams and goals.

Your mind can be free of 12-Step program indoctrination, and you can do things you have not had the time, energy, or breathing space to do in a long time. You can eat, sleep, clean your home, or read a book. You can recover what is *your life.*

I experienced NRA's very first attempts at *indoctrination* with the very first 12-Step program member I encountered. When I happened to mention a longtime friend had died tragically, the NRA blasted me with "How dare you be upset over something that is *God's will?!*" It was the first time in my entire life that anyone had taken the approach that I must give up my beliefs and adhere to *theirs.*

A quote from Adolph Hitler speaks volumes when it comes to 12-Step programs. *"If you tell a big enough lie and tell it often enough, it will be believed."* And it is something to consider, whether there are NRA's lying *to* you *or about* you.

12-Step programs can be in the past. The peace and hope they took away from you can be yours again. There is a way out-- "May you find it now."

Made in the USA
Lexington, KY
21 March 2015